DESIGN & YOU

YOUR GUIDE TO DECORATING WITH STYLE

A

REVELLI

PRODUCTION

DESIGN & YOU
Your Guide To Decorating With Style

By
CLARE REVELLI

With contributions by
Antonia Alexandra Klimenko

Design and Illusrations by
Dennis Redmond

Production Services by
Media Tech Enterprises, Inc.

For additional information please refer to page 94 or write:

REVELLI
1850 Union Street
San Francisco, CA 94123
415•673-6313

Every effort has been made to provide accurate color throughout this book. However, due to certain limitations in four-color printing, some discrepancies may occur. Therefore, color demonstrated in this book should be used only as a guideline.

A Revelli Production
Published by Revelli, 1850 Union Street,
San Francisco, CA 94123

First REVELLI trade paperback printing August 1992

ISBN: 0-960-8092-1-X

Printed in Mexico

DEDICATION

This book is dedicated to every individual seeking his or her personal design style!

ACKNOWLEDGEMENTS

With special appreciation to Dennis Redmond for his *divine design* and many talents…to Boris and Denise for their endless patience and colorful humor…to Lisa Davoren for her enthusiastic work/style…to Mel Owen for his wisdom and counsel…to Grant for his unique and innovative furniture designs…to Sophia for comprehending the word "deadline" at the tender age of three…and especially to Ilene Strober et al. at Woman's Day who made my dream of writing this book a reality!

…in memory of David Bradley Redmond, artist extraordinaire…

Clare Revelli in her
Dramatic Style
San Francisco home

ALSO BY CLARE REVELLI

COLOR & YOU

STYLE & YOU

BABY & YOU

THE COLORS OF YOUR LIFE

COLOR & YOU (*video*)

CONTENTS

INTRODUCTION

Today there are almost as many "ready-made" styles as there are people. In fact, developing your own personal style in the '90's can be all the more confusing because of the unlimited possibilities that exist. With so many "looks" that are woven into our culture, selection can be a difficult process if you lose the thread of **who you are** and **what works for you** in real life. For instance, your lifework—what you do and how you do it—may affect what you wear and how you present yourself and your home to others. Both personal style and lifestyle are part of your total image. And as time at home becomes more precious, there is an ever-increasing desire to fulfill both emotional and practical needs. When you walk through the door, dictated decorating style just doesn't feel as good as **your very own**.

DESIGN & YOU will help you identify and develop your own personal design style. It is your key to unlocking your own signature—a guide to discovering **you.** Style is being yourself on purpose, with the confidence to balance style and function, fashion and comfort. For whatever our style, all of us want to enjoy a meaningful space that's comfortable all year 'round. And because you know what you like best, you'll become your own best guide. The following sections are designed to help you with the building blocks to your decorating goal.

PART ONE

COLOR STYLE
PERSONAL STYLE
DESIGN STYLE

COOL • Summer & Winter

WARM • Spring & Autumn

SPRING *warm* SUMMER *cool*

AUTUMN *warm*   WINTER *cool*

COLOR SPECTRUM

The rainbow or "wheel of color" as it occurs in the sky is the basis for our own color spectrum or wheel. Understanding the natural order and positioning of color helps to provide us with the insight or "keys" to color relationship and harmony.

PRIMARY COLORS:

RED • passion and courage

YELLOW • cheerfulness and communication

BLUE • conscience and spirit

SECONDARY COLORS:

GREEN • abundance and faith

VIOLET • royalty and power

ORANGE • illumination and wit

COLOR STYLE

From the moment we open our eyes till the moment we close them, we experience the world in all its colored splendor. Nature's palette is everywhere: Spring with its bright and infectious shades of yellows and greens bursts forth in a fever of freshness and clarity. Summer unfolds in the peaceful pastel tones of translucent blues and pinks, creating a feeling of softness throughout. Autumn emerges with warm, muted earthen hues of rich golds and browns. Winter shines in the primary colors and the crisp dramatic contrasts of black and white. The climate, too, suggests warm and cool tones, affecting the way we dress as well as our decorating choices. And while seasons and climates inevitably change, as does our wardrobe, the color selections we make for our home are far more permanent. That is why it is so important to understand how to make good color decisions—to choose colors you can live with day in and day out, your **best** colors, colors that enhance not only the look of your home but the **feel** of it. The way you feel. In effect, you're choosing the way people feel and respond to you too. But first you need to develop a thorough awareness of how **you** respond to color. Whether we're aware of it or not, color has a powerful impact on our lives. It creates messages, establishes atmosphere and influences feelings. Down through history, colors have been given special meanings because of the particular images and feelings they evoke.

In the same way that we are affected by color, color affects our relationships with people. Even before we have exchanged a handshake with someone new, the colors he or she wears make an impression on us. If this person happens to be wearing his or her "best" colors, our subconscious forms a positive impression that says, "This person is in harmony." Unconsciously, unflattering colors create a negative response. So you see, color selection can be very emotional and personal, very subjective.

Have you ever noticed that most of the time the same colors you are intuitively attracted to are the very ones that flatter you most and seem to reflect your innate characteristics? Johannes Itten, one of the great colorists and teachers of all time, believed we prefer those colors most in harmony with our spiritual expression. He advanced the theory of seasonal color in which the most becoming colors for each person are those of one particular season.

The seasonal color system is based on the universally accepted cool-warm classification. The colors of your skin, hair and eyes are the primary keys to finding your seasonal style. Skin tone is the first and most important factor. A "Winter" or "Summer" seasonal type has skin that manifests a cool or blue undertone. A "Spring" or "Autumn" person has skin that shows a warm or golden undertone. This hardly narrows your selection, however, as color is almost limitless. So don't think you will have to give up the color blue because you are an Autumn. Just consider a 'warm' teal blue instead of a 'cool' royal blue. The key is all in the selection.

In essence, creating your own personal color palette means consciously recognizing what you've really known all along. Re-discovering your best colors will help you re-discover your natural glow. For color is a vital part of living. It is also one of the most effective decorating tools we have. Mastering its use will bring impact and dimension to your world and make everything brighter. Whoever could imagine, for instance, the magic of Disney's classic FANTASIA in an explosion of black and white? Or life for that matter? For color is magic. It sweeps across the world almost invisible surrounding us with a sense of well-being which influences our lives in very tangible ways. Ultimately, color provides a powerful means of personal transformation. It is no wonder, then, that people work most efficiently and play most joyously when surrounded by their own best subjective colors. Just as wearing them brings out the natural beauty that nature intended—being at home with your ideal colors allows you to be that much more at home with yourself. And when you are at home with yourself, isn't everybody?

Study the four seasonal models and color palettes in this section on color. They will assist you in better understanding the *cool/warm* classification and seasonal color concept.

If you would like to know more about the seasonal color concept as it relates to clothing, accessory and make up selections with your own inherent coloring—read **COLOR & YOU** by Revelli (see page 94).

SEASONAL COLOR PROFILES AND CHARACTERISTICS

SPRING

Spring people have a natural freshness, and an open, energetic informality. Their sunny energy is reflected in a palette that has great clarity of hue and is yellow-based. All of Spring's colors are **warm**.

SPRING PALETTE*

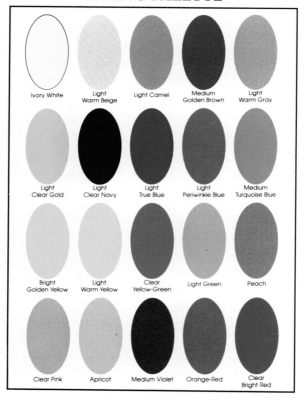

Ivory White	Light Warm Beige	Light Camel	Medium Golden Brown	Light Warm Gray
Light Clear Gold	Light Clear Navy	Light True Blue	Light Periwinkle Blue	Medium Turquoise Blue
Bright Golden Yellow	Light Warm Yellow	Clear Yellow-Green	Light Green	Peach
Clear Pink	Apricot	Medium Violet	Orange-Red	Clear Bright Red

*These are the twenty basic colors for a Spring person.
Depending upon an individual's varying characteristics,
lightened or darkened shades of these colors may be added.

12

SUMMER

Summer people have a fragile beauty. Simplicity and order create calm about them and this is shown in a color palette based on blue, the color of peace and quietude. All of Summer's colors are **cool.**

SUMMER PALETTE*

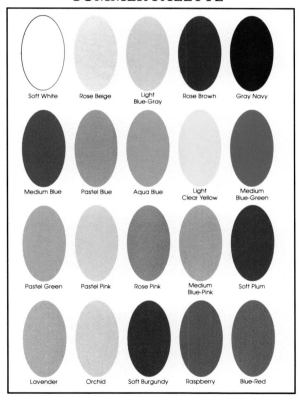

*These are the twenty basic colors for a Summer person. Depending upon an individual's varying characteristics, lightened tints or darkened shades of these colors may be added.

AUTUMN

Autumn people are a harvest of warmth. The independence and strength they show is echoed in the rich golden palette which glows about them. All of Autumn's colors are **warm.**

AUTUMN PALETTE*

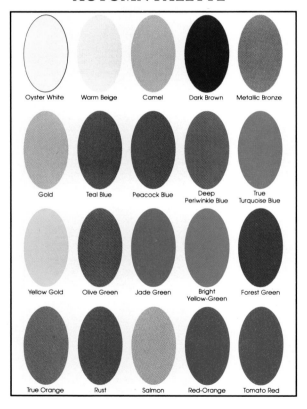

Oyster White	Warm Beige	Camel	Dark Brown	Metallic Bronze
Gold	Teal Blue	Peacock Blue	Deep Periwinkle Blue	True Turquoise Blue
Yellow Gold	Olive Green	Jade Green	Bright Yellow-Green	Forest Green
True Orange	Rust	Salmon	Red-Orange	Tomato Red

*These are the twenty basic colors for an Autumn person. Depending upon an individual's varying characteristics, lightened tints or darkened shades of these colors may be added.

WINTER

Winter people are persons of dramatic contrast, like a fine etching. Their coloring is decisive. Their palette is true and more primary than any of the other seasonal types. All of Winter's colors are **cool.**

WINTER PALETTE*

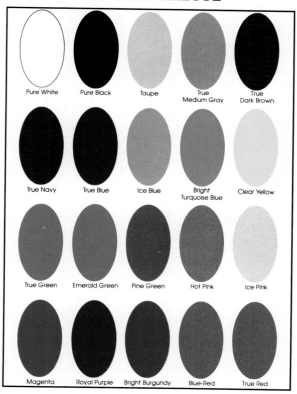

Pure White	Pure Black	Taupe	True Medium Gray	True Dark Brown
True Navy	True Blue	Ice Blue	Bright Turquoise Blue	Clear Yellow
True Green	Emerald Green	Pine Green	Hot Pink	Ice Pink
Magenta	Royal Purple	Bright Burgundy	Blue-Red	True Red

* These are the twenty basic colors for a Winter person. Depending upon an individual's varying characteristics, lightened tints or darkened shades of these colors may be added.

15

CLASSIC

NATURAL

DRAMATIC

ROMANTIC

If you would like to know more about your personal style as it relates to clothing, accessory and make up selections and your inherent taste, read **STYLE & YOU** by Revelli (see page 94).

PERSONAL STYLE

"The way you wear your hat, the way we danced till three, the memory of all that…no, no they can't take that away from me"
—Cole Porter

What is style? The dictionary defines it as a "manner of expression characteristic of an individual." But in essence the nature of style is not so easy to define or pin down. It seems to be that elusive quality like "charm" that makes one appear special— to stand apart from the crowd. Much in the same way we experience perfume and its essence, we experience the uniqueness of a person. Thus, if you are what you wear, then it follows that you are where you live. For style is how you present the inner you to the outer world. It goes beyond the superficial aspect of image. Indeed, it is your identity.

Where color may influence overall mood, style gives it shape. Like your mind and body, style is partly inherited, partly self-created. Cary Grant, widely known for his dapper style, once commented that "at a certain point in my early life, I decided what sort of person I wanted to be, and over the years I've become that person." And so you create your own style by understanding who you are and who you want to become. The person with style has consciously identified personal characteristics and ultimately shaped them into a unique language of behavior and appearance. And because it is a personal expression, true style is never right or wrong. Take Madonna, who will go to any fashion lengths. She's about as far from Chanel's classic chic as a person can get. Yet, both women will be remembered for a personal style that was absolutely right **for them.**

You cannot borrow a ready-made style as you would grab a coat right off the sales rack. Decorating with style means daring to be yourself. We have all been in homes that have told us more about the furniture than the personalities of the people who live there. Who are these people hiding behind stiffly ornamented screens and fashion-trend upholstery? Today there are as many furniture styles as there are lifestyles. With such a wide range of choices, it is easy to feel confused and frustrated—to lose confidence in ourselves and our ability to make pleasing, sensible choices. That is why no matter how wide the selection, the first thing to remember is that you will never get lost if you remember to ask yourself:

Who am I?

What am I most comfortable doing, wearing, being?

How do I want others to perceive me?

Just as all colors find their roots in the basic primaries of red, yellow and blue, you must never lose sight of who you are—your own primary likes and dislikes, your own way of doing and being. How you feel about yourself will influence your choice of furniture style, of which there are two major categories: **traditional** and **contemporary.** Traditional pieces were designed by master craftsmen of past generations, i.e.: Queen Anne, Chippendale, Louis XIV, etc. and are more formal in style. Contemporary means a style that is in common use today, adapted to modern methods of production and lifestyle. A "Natural" look (one of the five basic design styles we will discuss in the next chapter) would fall under this classification.

The other important factor to consider before making any decorating decisions is whether you want to have a **formal** or **informal** look to your home. All furniture is either formal or informal in its overall feeling, no matter what the period or style. Therefore, you have only to ask yourself, "Am I a more formal or informal type?" This basic exercise will help you to focus in on and better understand your own decorating preferences.

Sometimes, in order to find your own way, you have to go out of your way. Observe, absorb, experiment. Take chances. Living is an on-growing creative process, and we learn from our mistakes. The only real mistake is to discount our own feelings.

Here's something else to remember: Personal style and confidence go hand in hand. When you confide to yourself what pleases you most, you approach the world in a happier and more effective manner. In fact, the **only** way to develop a truly authentic personal style is to please yourself. When you are comfortable in a room the room is comfortable and real to others. And when it is real it is alive.

Everything is an extension of ourselves. Decorating with style gives us back energy and reaffirms what lives inside us as well as in the world around us. With a little vision and imagination this process is not only enlightening, it's fun! Thus, if you continue to embark on the journey of self-discovery, you will not only have an exciting adventure, you will become an adventure too!

TRADITIONAL

CONTEMPORARY

■ STYLE EVALUATIONS

To further assist you in discovering your dominant style type, you can take this thought-provoking quiz. Refer to the illustration on page 16 and the answer key following question #14.

1) MY PERSONAL STYLE TYPE IS:
   A) tailored, sophisticated, elegant
   B) trendsetting, exotic, artistic
   C) soft, poetic, unstructured
   D) casual, sporty, unpretentious
   E) free-spirited, versatile, innovative

2) THE SELECTION THAT BEST DESCRIBES MY PERSONALITY IS:
   A) charming and supportive
   B) energetic and outgoing
   C) understated and poised
   D) independent and diverse
   E) bold and confident

3) THE WOMAN WHOSE PERSONAL STYLE I MOST ADMIRE IS:
   A) Cher
   B) Goldie Hawn
   C) Jackie (Kennedy) Onassis
   D) Jane Seymour
   E) Gloria Steinem

4) THE MAN WHOSE PERSONAL STYLE I MOST ADMIRE IS:
   A) Kevin Kline
   B) Patrick Swayze
   C) Johnny Mathis
   D) Jeremy Irons
   E) Woody Allen

5) THE SELECTION THAT BEST DESCRIBES
MY CLOTHING PREFERENCE IS:
   A) comfortable/loose
   B) tailored/fitted
   C) architectural/contrasted
   D) detailed/layered
   E) a variety of styles from the above

6) THE SELECTION THAT BEST DESCRIBES
MY PREFERENCE IN LINE DESIGN IS:
   A) sharp/angular
   B) swirled/curled
   C) solid/straight
   D) waved/watered
   E) all of the above

7) THE SELECTION THAT BEST DESCRIBES
MY FABRIC PREFERENCE IS:
   A) soft, draped, flowing
   B) easy-care, natural fibers
   C) shiny, ornate, unusual
   D) woven, smooth matte finish
   E) all of the above

8) THE CHOICE THAT BEST DESCRIBES MY
PREFERENCE IN FLOWERS IS:
   A) roses, carnations or orchids
   B) antheriums, ginger or Bird of Paradise
   C) daisies, sunflowers or tulips
   D) baby's breath, violets or gardenias
   E) cactus flower, lily or mixed bouquet

9) THE SELECTION THAT BEST DESCRIBES
MY COLORS IS:
   A) soft pastels or tints
   B) earthy and muted
   C) neutral and subdued

D) bold and contrasting
E) varied and integrated

10) MY FAVORITE STYLE OF FURNITURE IS:
A) formal and traditional
B) informal, basic and country
C) contemporary, modern and unusual
D) detailed, Victorian
E) a combination of two or more of the above

11) THE FABRICS AND TEXTURES I ENJOY MOST IN MY HOME SURROUNDINGS ARE:
A) satins, velvets, silky woolens, suede cloths, chintz
B) soft sheers or wools, mohairs, damasks
C) tweeds, leather, hand-looms, rough linens, raw silks
D) crisp linens, gabardines, poplins
E) a combination of two or more of the above

12) THE SELECTION THAT BEST DESCRIBES MY SOFA PREFERENCE IS:
A) chaise longue
B) modular
C) tufted leather
D) plush velvet
E) overstuffed linen

13) THE SELECTION THAT BEST DESCRIBES MY PICTURE FRAME PREFERENCE IS :
A) walnut
B) tortoise shell
C) mirrored
D) white wicker
E) plexiglass

14) THE ADJECTIVE THAT BEST DESCRIBES
MY PERSONAL STYLE IS:
A) NATURAL
B) CLASSIC
C) ROMANTIC
D) DRAMATIC
E) ECLECTIC...(a combination of two or more of the
above)

Answer Key for Style Evaluations "N"-Natural, "C"-Classic,
"R"- Romantic, "D"-Dramatic, "E"-Eclectic :

1) a-C, b-D, c-R, d-N, e-E.
2) a-R, b-N, c-C, d-E, e-D.
3) a-D, b-N, c-C, d-R, e-E.
4) a-D, b-N, c-C, d-R, e-E.
5) a-N, b-C, c-D, d-R, e-E.
6) a-D, b-R, c-N, d-C, e-E.
7) a-R, b-N, c-D, d-C, e-E.
8) a-C, b-D, c-N, d-R, e-E.
9) a-R, b-N, c-C, d-D, e-E.
10) a-C, b-N, c-D, d-R, e-E.
11) a-D, b-R, c-N, d-C, e-E.
12) a-D, b-E, c-C, d-R, e-N.
13) a-C, b-N c-D, d-R, e-E.
14) Any answer is correct.

STYLE REVELL-ATIONS

1 RECOGNIZE...

Make a list of your likes and dislikes. Thumb through clothing catalogs and decorating magazines noting any styles that say "you." Study those pictures. What is it that you like about them? What don't you like? What would you like to change? How would you change it?

2 RE-THINK...

Don't accept everything at face value. Learn to find your own way by trusting in your own likes and dislikes. For instance:

a) If you like the "wrong" side of the fabric better than the "right" side—switch! The right side is always the one **you** like.

b) Who says you have to buy "drapes"? Sheets, for example, come in so many colors and patterns these designer days, there could be a style that's **you.** What's more, they are affordable and easy to throw in the wash.

3 RE-DO...

You like the shape of that table you inherited but not that dark oppressive finish? Do something about it! Try refinishing or stripping the wood. Perhaps you'll like the natural grain better; or paint it the color of **your** choosing. **Don't be afraid to make something your own. Personalize it.** What often catches the eye are accessories that reflect who you are—your lifestyle, your interests. **Display** the collection of folk art you've picked up in your travels. **Share** the abundance of flowers you've grown in your garden. These are both expressions of your enjoyment of living and they will inspire you as well as make the room feel more genuine to others.

4 RENEW...

Let go of the old and make room for the new! If you can't transform something to your liking—pass it on to an appreciative friend. You will both be glad you did. Getting on with your life is a great vehicle for **self-transformation**; an empty space provides the opportunity for you to discover who you are and what you **really** like.

DESIGN STYLE

"An outward and visible sign of an inward and spiritual grace"
—The Book of Common Prayer

There is good reason why home decorating is synonymous with interior design. For it is in your distinct attitude, the intention of your own inner personal spirit which translates an abstract vision into a specific physical environment. Just as color may sustain a theme or style, offering it space, design is an approach to style, giving it form and continuity. And while vision may give style direction, design takes us where we are going.

There are five basic and universal design styles, no matter what is currently in fashion. Each style has variations, but they are all individual personalities that have been developed. They are:

NATURAL

CLASSIC

ROMANTIC

DRAMATIC

ECLECTIC

THE NATURAL PROFILE

PERSONALITY:

Yours is an informal, approachable, down-to-earth style. Not unlike Mother Nature herself, you are inclined to draw upon your own resources in creating an environment of beauty and simplicity that will reflect the outdoors indoors. Unvarnished wood, terra cotta tile, open-weave fibers and fabrics always feel welcome in your natural setting of sunshine and daisies. And because such earth-tones as rusts, exuding a rich, mellow warmth, are typically used in this design style, an Autumn seasonal type, for instance, is likely to feel right at home.

LIFEWORK: *You might be...*
- an editor for a home decorating magazine
- a landscape designer
- in the healthcare profession
- activity director for a cruise line
- a restaurant chef

LIFESTYLE: *You might be found...*
- enjoying outdoor activities
- reading a book on gardening
- hosting a fundraising event
- in your jeep convertible
- in the non-smoking section

AMBIENCE:
- unadorned, simple, rustic, casual, unpretentious

DESIGN/STYLE:
- *An air of comfort*—whether robust country or rarefied city. Relaxed formality having nothing more to prove than "style can be easy"! All woods from light to dark and especially vintage mediums—cherry, pine, oak and maple. Wicker, willow and bamboo lend themselves especially well for your look. Antique brass and copper reflect your glowing personality. Braided, Berber, and sisal rugs and tactile textiles fit right into the genuine weave of things.

FLOWERS:
- Daisies, Sunflowers, Tulips...to name a few

DECORATING GOAL:
- To balance form and function without sacrificing inherent beauty and comfort.

THE CLASSIC PROFILE

PERSONALITY:

Yours is a formal, refined and timeless style. Trendy fads hold little interest to your discriminating tastes. You insist that the "dream" not only be credible, but that it lasts. You are adept at pulling together designs from another time to create or re-create an entire mood. You will wisely choose conservative and non-contrasting colors, surprise us with a few jewel-tones that help to authenticate a particular period, as well as shaded muted hues that evoke a bygone era. A Summer seasonal type could spend all their summers here!

LIFEWORK: *You might be...*
- an architect
- an antique watch dealer
- an investment counselor
- reading a book on etiquette
- attending an Ivy League school

LIFESTYLE: *You might be found...*
- sailing
- browsing at a fashionable boutique
- bidding at an estate sale
- playing tennis
- pruning your roses

AMBIENCE:
- formal, traditional, conservative, sophisticated, elegant

DESIGN STYLE:
- *A sure bet!* Ever correct and understated with soft, elegant curves interpreted by light to medium woods of traditional 18th and 19th century period English and American, as well as the painted and antiqued French and the more graceful contemporary. Because harmony is of prime importance...everything from polished surface to matte finish is skillfully blended to effect the calm overall time-honored essence.

FLOWERS:
- Roses, Carnations, Orchids...to name a few.

DECORATING GOAL:
- To make the most of each selection to reflect your total ideal forever after.

THE ROMANTIC PROFILE

PERSONALITY:

Yours is an unstructured, idyllic and expressive style. Fanciful and sentimental by nature, you combine rich emotional depth with charming diversity to convey an imaginative storybook setting—in which you are often the heroine or hero. With a longing and belonging in every corner, you wish only to delight, understand and comfort everything and everyone—notwithstanding yourself. And because a gentler spirit requires a light radiant palette, a delicate but exuberant Spring seasonal type might seek a little reassurance in the ROMANTIC'S cozy and sensuous surroundings!

32

LIFEWORK: *You might be...*

- a romance novelist
- an artist/fashion illustrator
- a musician/song lyricist
- working at a book store
- a homemaker wishing you were one of the above

LIFESTYLE: *You might be found...*

- planning a weekend rendezvous
- at the flea market
- taking part in a "Mystery Weekend"
- penning a love letter at your favorite cafe
- wearing a silk-tapestry vest

AMBIENCE:

- charming, gracious, evocative, fanciful, sentimental, thoughtful

DESIGN STYLE:

- **A personal expression** including everything from yester-year to yesterday —just as long as it's bright, whimsical and reminiscent of something or other! Delicate and more lightly scaled versions of country French, English, American as well as front-parlor or ice-cream-parlor Victorian, even fresh and fun-loving contemporary. Light to medium woods like walnut and ash and painted finishes offset the dense layering and patterning that abounds everywhere.

FLOWERS:

- Violets, Gardenias, Babies' Breath...to name a few

DECORATING GOAL:

- To organize your world of precious possessions so you can delight in it rather than be overcome by your surroundings.

THE DRAMATIC PROFILE

PERSONALITY:

Yours is a glamorous, artistic and progressive style. In fact, one that is taking a lifetime for you for create—as you invent and re-invent yourself along the way! Keenly aware of your surroundings, you never underestimate their use as a valuable tool in affecting the way people respond to you. Bold by nature, you are generally uncompromising. Frequently you see things as either black or white, which are, by the way, colors that you, unlike many, can employ successfully in your decor. Because a DRAMATIC color palette is one of clarity, vividness and sharp contrasts, a Winter seasonal type could steal the show!

34

LIFEWORK: *You might be...*
- in the entertainment field
- an illustrator/designer/copywriter
- dealing in real estate
- a trial lawyer
- in sales/marketing

LIFESTYLE: *You might be found...*
- at the movies
- visiting the museum of modern art
- hosting your own birthday bash
- at the record store—adding to your collection
- in a vintage clothing store buying a hat

AMBIENCE:
- bold, glamorous, artistic, exotic, progressive

DESIGN STYLE:
- **A little light opera**—always grand in both style and scale. Contrasting sharp, uncluttered lines and arresting stylized sophistication. Woods are dark and deep—highly lacquered or white and laminated. Avant Garde, modern, sleek with mirrored or chrome accents and featured object d'art.

FLOWERS:
- Ginger, Bird of Paradise, Anthuriums... to name a few.

DECORATING GOAL:
- To create a memorable space in which to highlight each individually decorated corner.

THE
ECLECTIC
PROFILE

PERSONALITY:

Yours is a creative melding of the best of all the styles. Whereas the rest of us can cross over to the other basic design styles from time to time, you seem to have incorporated them into your very consciousness, selecting and interpreting a style at will in your own unique way. Because you are a risk-taker at heart, and don't like too many limitations, you are bound to select from a wide range of design and color. Seeking the best of both worlds, you are, of course, a person for all seasons!

LIFEWORK: *You might be...*
- in the video field
- a documentary producer-director
- in the healing arts
- a teacher
- an interior designer

LIFESTYLE: *You might be found...*
- embarking on new adventure
- taking a philosophy class
- reading an article on acupressure
- donating time and money to your favorite cause
- recycling

AMBIENCE:
- integrated, free-spirited, versatile, innovative, reaffirming

DESIGN STYLE:
- *An exciting adventure!* Because you understand that even the most diverse elements share a common ground, you are able to successfully contrast traditional and contemporary furnishings, often by placing them in delightful juxtapositions that adds to rather than detracts from the unifying whole. Being one of a kind yourself, it's not surprising that you appreciate furnishings that are of a diverse and unusual mode.

FLOWERS:
- Lilies, Cactus-flowers, mixed-bouquets...to name a few.

DECORATING GOAL:
- To find the link with others that will ultimately distinguish you from others.

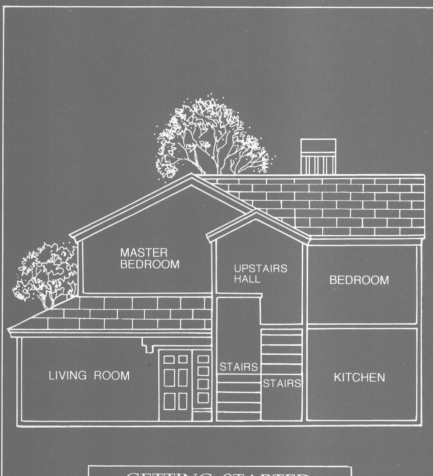

MASTER BEDROOM

UPSTAIRS HALL

BEDROOM

LIVING ROOM

STAIRS

STAIRS

KITCHEN

GETTING STARTED

PART TWO

HOW TO GET STARTED
BEFORE YOU BEGIN!

HOW TO GET STARTED BEFORE YOU BEGIN!

"An interior is the natural projection of the soul..."
—Coco Chanel

Here are a few thought-provoking questions, reaffirmations and helpful pointers intended to encourage you to make a self-evaluation and more-over, to use your imagination towards a practical decorating end.

I. TAKING INVENTORY

1) My dominant overall feeling is best expressed as _____

2) I can see myself crossing over to a _____ or _____ design style from time to time.

3) My ideal or best colors are _____ and _____

4) My favorite combinations of colors are _____ and _____

5) Make a list of your rooms. What kind of "feeling" do you want each room to have?

6) What is the function of each room? What kind of activities do you enjoy there?
What kind of activity would you like to be able to enjoy there that you are not presently?

7) Make a list of those possessions:
A. you will definitely use in your new decorating scheme
B. you must change or modify in order to enjoy
C. you may store, sell or pass on to others

II. REALITY CHECK

8) How much money can I allot to the decorating of each room?_____

9) Knowing the difference between what you can't change and what you can.

   A. **Climate** is often a significant factor. If you live in a warm climate your furniture may be lighter in both wood tone and weight. If you live in a cool climate, furniture may be heavier and darker in wood tone.

   B. **Natural light** (or lack of) may indicate what type of activity you may or may not engage in. If you enjoy painting, for instance, natural light cannot be substituted with artificial. Therefore, choosing the right room or space for that particular activity is important.

   C. **Space.** Understanding the function of a wall is key to determining how much space you really have. Does that wall perform an important function besides the obvious ones of holding up the ceiling or strengthening the foundation? Sometimes a wall can be removed, offering more space, better light, greater decorating possibilities. Consult a professional who can establish **real** boundaries. **Consult yourself** to better understand which *walls* are self-imposed.

10) Always **make** space for your lifework/lifestyle. If you don't please yourself, you won't please anybody. Say the living room has the best light, space and focal point for your handloom. Don't be afraid to set up shop there. Visit with others while you work! Hang your weavings on your walls. Combine your workspace with your living space. Or, take over the entire room and combine the living room with the dining room or adjacent area. **Don't** let the words "living room" or "dining room" dictate its use to you. **Don't** be afraid to let the rooms work for you. **Don't** get hemmed in by your own boundaries. **Do** make every room a **living** room!

III. IMAGINATION: YOUR BEST NATURAL RESOURCE

11) Imagine the room you want to decorate is empty. If you could have any furnishing or decorating item…
   A. what would it be?
   B. where would you place it?
   C. would it be the focal point of the room? (i.e. the point of interest that first attracts the eye)
   D. where do you see yourself in relation to it? (i.e. where would you place yourself—in the center of the room, alongside the wall, or near the window?)

12) **Try moving things around. Begin inside your head**— the best place to start. Ask yourself: "Am I getting the optimum use of each furnishing in its existing placement or would it provide me with more function and/or comfort in a different room or space? Often the process of learning is un-learning or undoing. Don't forget to reassess possibilities as your life and needs evolve.

13) **Imagination:** your guide to style.
   Who has it: The person living in a small, dark room with no window who will put up a painting or a poster depicting a view and make drapes for it on either side!
   Who doesn't: the person who lives in a mansion and employs someone else to pick out all the furnishings complete with "personal touches."

IV. PERSONAL TOUCHES

14) **Effect a feeling.** Although it is true that some accessories, like furniture can cost more than you are willing to spend, there are some things that you can do quite inexpensively that might effect the same or similar feeling. For instance:
   A. If that dramatic sculpture you've been desiring is inclined to make a dramatic dent in your pocketbook—consider, instead, reshaping your own approach to the art objects you already have. Providing individual spotlighting for each painting that lines your hallway will make each rendering look important and add that element of drama.

B. Fabric with a floral motif can make you feel as if you're in a garden. Try adding a few potted flowers resembling the fabric. Or, if you **do** have a terrace ...fill it with vines and blooms that will provide a living expression of the floral motif.

15) **Reflect an interest.** Not everyone can afford an abundance of original artwork. So...maybe you'll frame those memorable theatre playbills and group them collectively on the wall behind your piano or entertainment unit.

•DECORATING NOTE•

Grouping small and similar items together will often help to unify a theme. One small item on its own can often look lost or insignificant. Two the same size may have to fight for attention. **Exception to the rule**: When two improbable items are paired to provide a point of interest and an interplay of irreverent wit. (see ECLECTIC)

---

16) **Engage the room in dialogue.** Ask yourself again: What kind of feeling do I want each room to have? Reflection and contentment, activity and creativity? A little whimsy and romance? Remember the elements of every room must engage in a degree of dialogue. It is the relationship or interplay of one element to another that conveys contrast or similarity: The antique framed fan on the wall echoed by the similar fan pattern on the sheets. The dramatic contrast of red sofa and chairs to stark white walls. Don't forget to engage **yourself** in the dialogue. By letting your own wardrobe both reaffirm and offset the theme, you can become a living extension of a room. For instance, if you are drawn to geometric patterns (in furniture style or fabric), you might want to employ a similar or contrasting pattern in a caftan or lounging robe. This adds the connecting thread linking you to the original decorating plan—your perfect end result.

V. MAKING PLANS

17) Take pen to paper and make a working plan for each room you intend to redecorate or modify, taking into consideration the following:
- **Climate** (cool vs. warm weather)
- **Light** (natural vs. artificial)
- **Space** (existing and potential)
- **Purpose** (i.e. : sleeping, sitting, creative space, recreation, office etc.)
- **Color** (cool or warm based on activity or feeling you wish to complement or evoke)
- **Budget** (time and money)
- **Decorating goal:**_____

_____

_____

_____

Jot down any additional ideas you may have that will inspire you to get started before you begin! _____

_____

_____

_____

_____

_____

_____

_____

PART THREE

BASIC TRAINING:

FORMAL VS. INFORMAL
FIVE DESIGN STYLES
TRANSITIONS
SETTING THE STAGE

FORMAL VS. INFORMAL

To better understand each of the five design styles—NATURAL, CLASSIC, ROMANTIC, DRAMATIC, ECLECTIC, — you must first identify the unique and elemental characteristic of each as well as recognize the similarities and differences amongst all of them.

Just as there are two major classifications of color—cool and warm—there are also two major classifications of furniture design: **formal** and **informal**. These words are not absolutes as there is no such thing as the most formal or the ultimate informal room.

It's also important to understand that certain "tricks of the trade" can reverse the formal and informal rules in decorating. For instance, one could choose the exact same style of sofa and cover it in two completely different fabrics. A smooth satin-striped taffeta would make this piece appear formal. However, the same sofa covered in a nubby natural-weave linen would label it informal. So it is often a matter of the fabric selection which determines the overall formal or informal feeling in the room. This applies to everything from sofas to beds to wall and window treatments where the fabric can be so widely varied. Of course continuity with this 'feeling' must exist throughout the entire room in order for it to be classified properly.

Just as all people have distinct characteristics which identify them, so, too, does a style relate to design characteristics identifying the work of a famous designer or school of designers. Often furniture styles are classified as either "traditional" (classic or period) or "contemporary" (country or modern). Today's furniture descends largely from the great styles of the 17th and 18th century. Since it was during this "period" of time in history that particular monarchs or governments reigned, the terms period or style are used interchangeably. Therefore, Sheraton, Hepplewhite, William and Mary, etc. are names borne by traditional furniture of that period of time. These traditional styles are frequently used in more "formal" settings.

Some factors that might tend to make a room more **formal** are:

cool colors
traditional or period styles
smooth surfaced woods and fabrics

symmetrical arrangements
sculptured rugs
wall moldings

Likewise, some factors that might tend to make a room more **informal** are:

warm colors
contemporary or country styles
heavily textured fabrics

asymmetrical arrangements
matting on the floors
ceramics, earthenware items

The major difference between any formal or informal furniture pieces has to do with the actual details, materials used and the craftsmanship applied. The cost can also be affected by these elements.

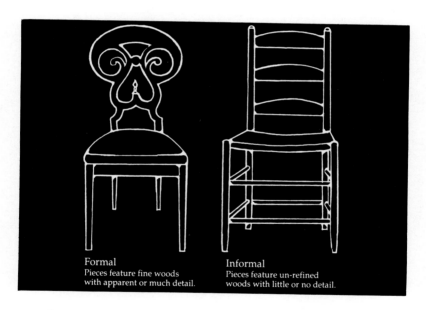

Formal
Pieces feature fine woods
with apparent or much detail.

Informal
Pieces feature un-refined
woods with little or no detail.

Contemporary designers are actually descendants of the traditional line, having taken the formal design and evolved it into a comfortable interpretation. Contemporary styles are often found in the "informal" settings.

Whether your look is formal or informal, traditional or contemporary, it is important to understand the differences and recognize the one that works best for your own design style.

THE
NATURAL
ROOM

■ NATURAL

COLORS: Warm

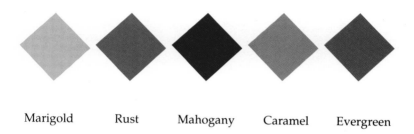

| Marigold | Rust | Mahogany | Caramel | Evergreen |

Additional suggestions: Warm Beige, Salmon, Oyster White, Bright Yellow-Green, Teal Blue, Persimmon...plus the warm Personal Palettes of spring and autumn; all compromise colors.

STYLE ESSENCE: Informal

What you see is what you get. Native woods formerly suited to the needs of peasant folk—(thus the term "country")—centered in appreciation of its own vertical spirit. Efficient, sturdy, basic and functional. Solid, square, unpretentious in its simplicity of line and decoration.

DESIGN STRATEGY:

Because you are a NATURAL you can take your cue from nature, which abounds with decorating clues. Colors and accessories inspired by your own surroundings are more inclined to beautify and enhance the interior of your home.

■ NATURAL ACCESSORIES

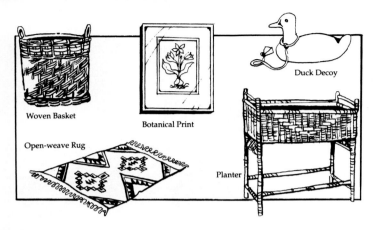

Woven Basket

Botanical Print

Duck Decoy

Open-weave Rug

Planter

■ NATURAL FURNITURE

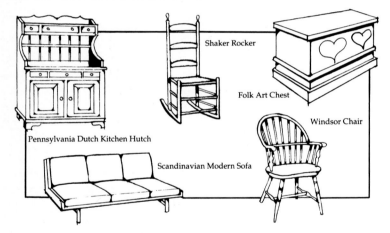

Shaker Rocker

Folk Art Chest

Windsor Chair

Pennsylvania Dutch Kitchen Hutch

Scandinavian Modern Sofa

Additional NATURAL Accessories:

Leather-bound books, Audubon and botanical prints, Navajo rugs, East Indian Kelims, earthenware, afghans, folk art, brass candlesticks, mother-of-pearl chests, baskets, dried herbs and flowers, decoys, early American wooden spools for candlesticks, tin milk jugs, oil lamps, antique collectible porcelain dolls, wooden towel racks.

Additional NATURAL Furniture:

American Colonial, Arts and Crafts, Country and Frontier, French Country, Gothic, Mission, Pennsylvania Dutch, Ranch Style, Scandinavian Modern, Shaker, Southwest, Urban Primitive.

■ NATURAL

WINDOW TREATMENTS: Wallpaper or hand-stenciled shade, cafe-style shutters, single wooden rod with plain cafe drapes

FABRICS: Rough linen, 100% cotton and wool, corduroy, canvas, old homespun, calico, muslin, denim, madras plaid, ticking, tweed, gingham, seersucker, camel hair, mohair, velvet, suede, cowhide, and hand-loomed.
Patterns/Texture: Quilted, paisley, nature or botanical motifs, plaids, checks, polka dots, folk art, hand-stenciled. Flat, matte, dull, rough, brushed or crinkled finishes preferred.

LIGHTING: Brass table lamps, chandeliers of brass, pewter, wood or metal, brass and tin lanterns, candleholders, hurricane lamps, stenciled or pottery-base lamps.
Enlightenment: Diffused light by soft white bulbs will blend well with your decor, giving it a natural glow.

WALL DETAILS: Stenciled, plain; wood-grain panels; miniature-print wallpaper

FLOORS: All natural grain woods, unvarnished, stripped and plain. Area rugs such as Indian, Dhurrie, rag, hooked, braided or handpainted/stenciled floorcloths. Wall-to-wall Berber, Sisal, rope; maize or seagrass scatter mats. Brick, cement, stone or slate. Terra cotta, ceramic or hand-painted tiles

WOODS/STAINS: All 'blonde' woods; walnut and mahogany, light oak, birch or ash; maple, redwood, red mahogany, pine, elm.

METALS: Antiqued gold, brass, bronze, copper; black or brown wrought iron; tin.

■ NATURAL

DO:
- try gold for a sophisticated yet natural glow
- select nature patterns and textured fabrics
- invest in earthenware, pottery and ceramics
- display an abundance of flowers—both fresh and dried
- invite "garden furniture" into the comfort of your home

DON'T:
- underestimate your need for natural light
- choose a color that will "take over" the room

DECORATING TIP:

"Spring" flowers, "Autumn" prints and other details that you can rotate will make any room come alive with every season.

NATURAL BEDROOM

NATURAL LIVING ROOM

THE
CLASSIC
ROOM

■ CLASSIC

COLORS: Cool

Sky Blue   Gray Fog   Orchid   Rose Pink   Aquamarine

Additional suggestions: Soft White, Light Burgundy, Rose Beige, Soft Plum, Blue-Red...plus the cool Personal Palettes of summer and winter; all compromise colors.

STYLE ESSENCE: Formal

A restrained balance of beauty and symmetry. Because it is the essence of harmony, the lyre—also celebrated for its form—is often represented in formal furniture styles. Curves are simple but elegant. Straight lines echoed in columns theme.

DESIGN STRATEGY:

Because you are a CLASSIC, your design style has every intention of lasting you a lifetime. Therefore, it is important for you to choose all of the right elements in order to achieve the kind of harmony and balance you can live with. Let the room evolve slowly.

■ CLASSIC ACCESSORIES

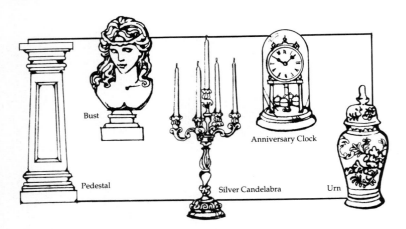

Bust

Pedestal

Silver Candelabra

Anniversary Clock

Urn

■ CLASSIC FURNITURE

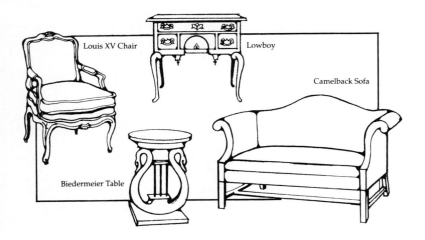

Louis XV Chair

Lowboy

Camelback Sofa

Biedermeier Table

Additional CLASSIC Accessories:

A dark mahogany or walnut highboy, most fine antiques, marble pedestals and plant stands, fine porcelain, silver, rose-gold lamp bases, throw pillows in stripes and paisleys, a silver tea set, floral motifs, pettipoint foot stool, brass sconce, tilt table, oriental cache pot, Grandfather's clock, globe/stand.

Additional CLASSIC Furniture:

Adam Brothers, Biedermeier, Chippendale, Empire and Regence, Federal, French Classic, Georgian, Hepplewhite, Louis XIII through XVI, Queen Anne, Sheraton.

■ CLASSIC

WINDOW TREATMENTS: Full length draperies with swag valance, tie-backs & underlayer sheers, floor length Austrian shades , traditional pleated Roman shade.

FABRICS: Shantung silk, linen woven cotton, wool, sheer, floral brocades, English Garden chintz, rayon damask, satin, taffeta, tartan, mohair, cashmere, crushed velvet, ultra suede, quality leather.
Patterns/Textures: Moiré, shaded patterns, tartan plaids, large florals, documentary-reproduction prints, striped satins and taffetas, shirt patterns; pinstripes, pin dots, foulards, herringbones and understated prints. Glazed, smooth, matte or slight sheen finishes.

LIGHTING: Crystal, brass and metal chandeliers, porcelain table and antique porcelain candelabras, wall sconces, bankers' lamps, recessed lighting and picture lights.
Enlightenment: A chandelier hanging from the center of the ceiling can provide an interesting focal point, especially for a room that has no architectural detail.

WALL DETAILS: Wood-grain paneling, murals, wainscoting; historical and family heritage collectibles; grass cloth; woven and textured wallpaper; glazed, marbled, or stippled finishes.

FLOORS: Bare varnished hardwood floors; old and new wall-to-wall carpets; Oriental, Persian, Turkish or Tibetan rugs; marble or Terrazzo tile.

WOODS/STAINS: Solid cherry, dark pine, walnut or mahogany, oak. Dark woods preferred over light, varnished rather than stripped or unfinished.

METALS: Silver, pewter, chrome, white or rose gold, brass.

■ CLASSIC

DO:
- make a few choice selections over several inferior ones
- relax the formality enough so you can enjoy it
- make purchases from experienced reputable dealers
- authenticate by giving attention to detail
- go to auctions to improve your discerning eye

DON'T:
- overlook climate in selecting dark vs. light woods
- paint anything in bold colors unless you can live with it

DECORATING TIPS:

An entire wall of books can provide many dashes of color. Keep adding contemporary classics to traditional, and see how many new colors and ideas you can turn up in time.

CLASSIC DINING ROOM

CLASSIC LIVING ROOM

THE ROMANTIC ROOM

■ ROMANTIC

COLORS: Warm

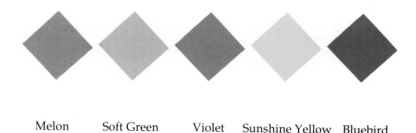

Melon   Soft Green   Violet   Sunshine Yellow   Bluebird

Additional suggestions: Ivory White, Light Clear Gold, Peach, Clear Rosy Red, Light Camel...plus the warm Personal Palettes of spring and autumn; all compromise colors.

STYLE ESSENCE: Informal

Less restrained than classic, but with a halo of respectability and charm. Its whimsical curve embraces the substantial oval, round and horseshoe shapes as well as light and intricate expressions of intimacy and sentimentality. Though the ROMANTIC will employ "formal" furnishings the mood is relaxed due to the ROMANTIC'S open display of affection.

DESIGN STRATEGY:

Because you are a ROMANTIC, your decorating concern will be that you give your rooms just the right feeling. One has only to look at your personal belongings to understand that they remain some of your most important decorating accessories. They should, in fact, help indicate to you which way to proceed.

■ ROMANTIC ACCESSORIES

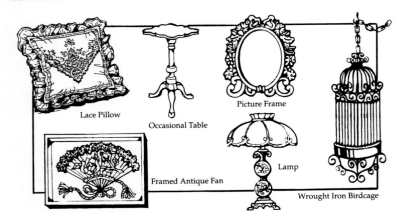

Lace Pillow

Occasional Table

Picture Frame

Framed Antique Fan

Lamp

Wrought Iron Birdcage

■ ROMANTIC FURNITURE

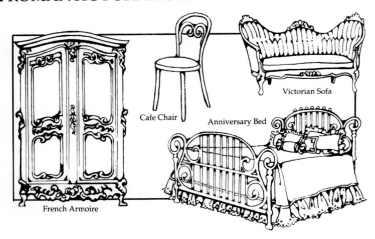

Cafe Chair

Anniversary Bed

Victorian Sofa

French Armoire

Additional ROMANTIC Accessories:

Armoires, hat-trees, screens with animated floral motifs, pillows of lace and ruffles, polished brass fireplace fans, hand-loomed rag rugs, soft quilts and plush throws, lavender scents and cameos. Ribbon and lace-trimmed picture frames, crocheted glove and antique jewelry collections, hand painted fans, porcelain figurines.

Additional ROMANTIC Furniture:

Art Nouveau, Chippendale and Hepplewhite, Duncan Phyfe, fanciful and curvy wrought iron and wicker, French Country, French Regence, Italian and French, less massive and heavily curved Queen Anne, Louis XV, XVI, Provincial, Victorian.

■ ROMANTIC

WINDOW TREATMENTS: Tie-back floor length sheers with smocked valance, full Bishop floor length draperies with swag valance and sheer underlayer, Austrian shade with swag draped valance.

FABRICS: Gossamer, chiffon, tissue linen batiste, organza, lace, dotted Swiss, eyelet, rayon voile, challis, polished cotton, sheer wool or crepe, jersey, peau de soie, angora, cashmere, velvet.
Patterns/Textures: Small floral or garden prints, miniature dots, flowers, hearts or animated prints; impressionist designs. Smooth, soft, subtle sheen or translucent finishes.

LIGHTING: Candles, cut-glass candleholders, Tiffany lamps, standing and table lamps draped with lace or gossamer fabric, lamps with glass and porcelain and filigree bases. Crystal or frosted glass chandeliers.
Enlightenment: Put a dimmer on as many light fixtures as you can to allow for your many moods.

WALL DETAILS: Trompe l'oeil; tiny floral print wallpaper; flower stenciling; moiré (watermark) dragging; fabric covered walls. Memorabilia; photos of family and friends embellished with lace matting.

FLOORS: Thick, plush wall-to-wall carpets; needlepoint area rugs; hand painted ceramic tiles in floral patterns; wood in stenciled pastel colors; trompe l'oeil.

WOODS/STAINS: All blond woods, light or dark oak, pine, elm, ash or walnut; old oak, pickled pine, beech and birchwood, light mahogany; white wicker or woven rattan.

METALS: Highly polished gold or filigree brass, white or black carved wrought iron

■ ROMANTIC

DO:
- display keepsakes in a curio cabinet
- indulge yourself with layers of sensuous fabric
- build yourself a window seat—for day-dreaming, of course
- borrow a color scheme from a French impressionistic painting

DON'T:
- sacrifice your comforts for "looks"
- clutter—unless it's **by design.**

DECORATING TIP:

Paint each room a different variation of the same shade (i.e. pink, lavender, rose). This will help to unify, while contrasting the colors will offer the fantasy and diversity you seek.

ROMANTIC BEDROOM

ROMANTIC DINING ROOM

THE
DRAMATIC
ROOM

■ DRAMATIC

COLORS: Cool

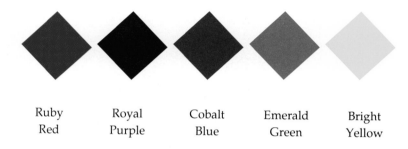

Ruby	Royal	Cobalt	Emerald	Bright
Red	Purple	Blue	Green	Yellow

Additional suggestions: Bright White, Gloss Black, Icy Blue, Magenta, Hot Pink...plus the cool Personal Palettes of summer and winter; all compromise colors.

STYLE ESSENCE: Formal

A dichotomy of striking proportions. Either the graceful winding curves of an Art Nouveau vein or the daring hard-edged sleek of glass and chrome. Both are equally memorable interpretations of a design style whose overextended and exaggerated line gives it movement and drama.

DESIGN STRATEGY:

Because you are a DRAMATIC you will go out of your way to be yourself. Since decorating is just a formalized progression of your personal style—maximize your star potential by featuring **yourself** as the most important accessory in your own set design.

■ DRAMATIC ACCESSORIES

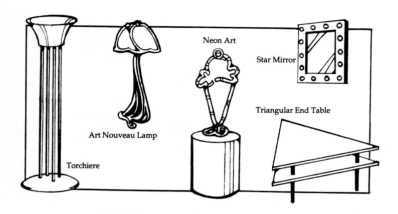

Neon Art

Star Mirror

Triangular End Table

Art Nouveau Lamp

Torchiere

■ DRAMATIC FURNITURE

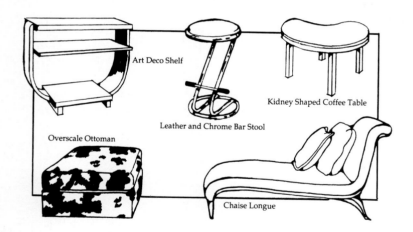

Art Deco Shelf

Kidney Shaped Coffee Table

Leather and Chrome Bar Stool

Overscale Ottoman

Chaise Longue

Additional DRAMATIC Accessories:

Crystal chandeliers and vases, shiny picture frames of glass and chrome, Coromandel screens, movie memorabilia, cube or parsons tables, experimental and sculptured art, butterfly chairs, quartz wall clock, Hi-tech table and bar ware, free-form vases and objects d'art, glass and chrome occasional tables or bar carts.

Additional DRAMATIC Furniture:

Art Deco, Art Nouveau, Bauhaus, Egyptian, High-Tech, Mediterranean, Memphis, Mission, Modern, Oriental, Spanish Renaissance, Utility.

■ DRAMATIC

WINDOW TREATMENTS: Single floor length swag with rope tie-back, knotted floor length swag with gathered drapes, contrasting color mini-blinds with cloth valance.

FABRICS: Sateen silk, satin and taffetas, metallic lame, heavy damask and brocade, double knit, patterned velveteen and velour, faille, leopard or zebra animal faux fur
Patterns/Textures: Large prints, geometrics, polka dots, stripes and checks; linear and bold designs, animal prints with striking two-color contrasts. Shiny, glittery, tightly woven and lighter reflective finishes.

LIGHTING: Art Deco style or geometrically shaped sconces, floor canister uplights and ceiling track lighting with theatrical spots, Art Nouveau table lamps, metal and glass standing (torchiere) lamps, wrought iron or shiny enamel candlesticks, lucite and metal floor and table lamps, contemporary crystal chandeliers.
Enlightenment: Discover the many new fluorescent, incandescent and low-voltage bulbs that are energy efficient as well as flattering to skintones.

WALL DETAILS: Abstract, asymmetrical and graphic wallcoverings in bold and contrasting color combinations; glossy, glazed and avant garde paint finishes; mirrored walls or displays of oversized contemporary art work.

FLOORS: Wood parquet high-gloss, painted or lacquered; industrial or sculptured pile carpet; abstract design area rugs; vinyl ; terrazzo or ceramic tile; black/white.

WOODS/STAINS: Dark wood; mahogany, walnut or teak. Colored stains, painted enamel, lacquered wood.

METALS: Shiny chrome, silver , platinum or white gold.

■ DRAMATIC

DO :
- emphasize opulence with exotic and luxurious props
- position your sofa at an angle
- mirror an entire wall for dazzle and dimension
- consider painting a wall in two contrasting colors
- coordinate your wardrobe with your decor

DON'T:
- let an eyesore upstage you—toss it
- play down anything you can play up

DECORATING TIP:

Try painting one wall of every room a different color. Leave the other three white for contrast and that touch of drama.

DRAMATIC BEDROOM

DRAMATIC BEDROOM

THE
ECLECTIC
ROOM

■ ECLECTIC

COLORS: Neutral, Cool or Warm

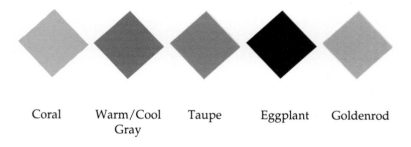

| Coral | Warm/Cool Gray | Taupe | Eggplant | Goldenrod |

Additional suggestions: Deep Periwinkle Blue, Dark Coffee-Bean Brown, Sandalwood Beige, Olive Green, Yellow Mustard Gold...plus seasonal Personal Palettes; compromise colors.

STYLE ESSENCE: FORMAL /INFORMAL:
Incorporating all elements of form, line and color, ECLECTIC provides the crossroads for all design styles. Thus, its effect is to pull one in two directions: It reassures with the familiar at the same time it disarms with the innovative. That is **why** ECLECTIC is an on-groing evolution.

DESIGN STRATEGY:
Because you are an ECLECTIC you usually have a purpose but don't always know where you are going. Since every journey begins with one step—try focusing on a theme. Then you will have a point of reference to serve as your constant, which you can approach from as many directions as you desire.

■ ECLECTIC ACCESSORIES

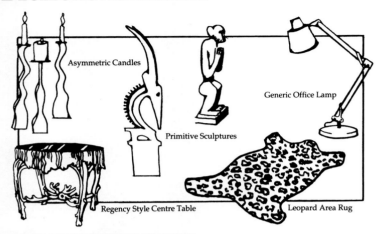

Asymmetric Candles

Generic Office Lamp

Primitive Sculptures

Regency Style Centre Table

Leopard Area Rug

■ ECLECTIC FURNITURE

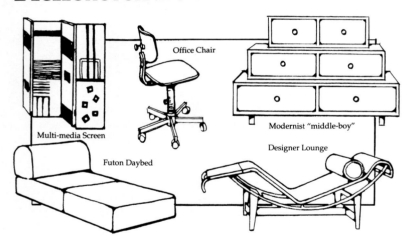

Office Chair

Multi-media Screen

Futon Daybed

Modernist "middle-boy"

Designer Lounge

Additional ECLECTIC Accessories:

Primitive and modern art; sculpture or things possessing sculptural quality; personal expressions; collages, one-of-a-kind objects; statues of Buddha; shoji screens, ethnic costumes and tribal masks; a combination wood and mirrored coffee table, possibly featuring mosaic tile; anything old, authentic in origin.

Additional ECLECTIC furniture:

All furniture styles may be included here. Ones of particular interest are: Art Deco, Art Moderne, Art Nouveau, Bauhaus, Biedermeier, Modern Metal, Urban Primitive, Utility.

■ ECLECTIC

WINDOW TREATMENTS: Wooden vertical blinds, full length swag drapes twisted and knotted in a free form style, single fabric swag combined with Japanese rice paper shades.

FABRICS: Lots of diverse combinations: velvet with leather; suede with silk; linen with lace; organza, wool, silk, polished cotton, durable sailcloth, gauze, sculptured velvet, knit, brocade, antique satin and taffeta, Surah.
Patterns/Textures: International, primitive and ethnic prints; plain sheers to intricate tapestries, moiré, Batik and paisley designs; two or three prints combined. Matte to shiny, opaque to transparent finishes.

LIGHTING: Ginger jar lamps, track, floor canister uplights, halogen, wall-mounted swing-arm lamps, mercury vapor lights, votive candles, suspended fixtures of glass, porcelain or metal; neon.
Enlightenment: A canister uplight placed on the floor and aimed at a corner bookshelf or plant will add texture, dimension and depth to any room.

WALL DETAILS: Murals, tapestries, one-of-a-kind artworks or an oversized wall hanging; lots of 'collectibles' in various sizes and combinations.

FLOORS: Wood flooring of all types. Area rugs in Numdah, Dhurrie, Indian, Oriental and Flokati. Kelims of Afghan and Turkish origin. All types of matting: sisal, rope, rush, seagrass. Mosaic or primitive-motif ceramic tiles.

WOODS/STAINS: All woods and stains, light to dark; maple, mahogany, walnut, oak, cherry, pine, birch or beech. Painted wicker and rattan.

METALS: Gold, silver, copper, bronze.

■ ECLECTIC

DO:
- choose flooring wisely for the not-so-common denominator
- take a decorating risk—it's just your style!
- indulge yourself with an art object or
- own at least one glass table—it goes with everything
- re-arrange the furniture to gain new perspective

DON'T:
- throw everything together and expect it to work
- disregard your inherent seasonal colors

DECORATING TIP:

Expressing yourself through a variety of style preferences is your hallmark. Whether it's a traditional Biedermeier table married to a contemporary Eames chair or three different area rugs gracing your bedroom, you embrace both the past and the present.

ECLECTIC LIVING ROOM

ECLECTIC LIVING ROOM

TRANSITIONS

As you can see, style rarely just happens—design never! When you come to realize that your life is a work in progress, you begin to understand that design, too, is a process which requires an on-going awareness and the willingness to change. The ECLECTIC especially, must learn to recognize and compare style characteristics before refining and translating them into her own unique way of using them. But, in truth, **each** design group must have a meaningful balance to achieve a successful decorating mix.

These design profiles are, at best, a point of reference that can help you to identify and organize your own likes and dislikes. Remember: the best way to get to know yourself is to ask questions. The more specific the question—the more specific the answer. And because no two people are alike, who better than you to throw the spotlight on your own uniqueness!

For instance, by identifying your **dominant** look, you can cross over to another design style to create your own individual trademark. A summer seasonal type might feel as comfortable as a spring in a ROMANTIC setting, implemented with muted pastels instead of clear ones. Accessories can instantly alter your primary image, too. A CLASSIC room becomes a ROMANTIC one with the addition of a Victorian quilt, ruffled lace curtains and a cameo portrait. A NATURAL setting turns DRAMATIC when a stunning sculpture or large exotic plant is presented in the foreground under theatrical lighting. A generic sofa makes a great transitional piece as anything you want it to be. Cover it in a rich burgundy brocade and top it off with elegant and traditional tassel pillows and you have a CLASSIC piece. Cover it in periwinkle blue-and-white striped linen and you've created a perfect bridge for your NATURAL to CLASSIC contemporary decor.

Finding the common denominator is like finding the missing link. Just when you think you're lost, it opens up new and exciting avenues. The trick, of course, is to approach **each** decorating crossroad with a guiding vision of your overall style. Once you know who you are (your best colors and personal style) and where you are going (your design destination), you will experience a pleasure and personal satisfaction that money can't buy. After all, what could be better than finding your way home!

NATURAL CLASSIC ROMANTIC DRAMATIC ECLECTIC

SETTING THE STAGE

"Crossing over" or integrating design styles is often a natural process. Here are a few examples to assist you in your understanding of how you might "effect a feeling" on purpose. Refer to the "crossover" photos on pages 82 to 83 and to the answer key following question #6.

1 You have several small photographs which you would like to display, and in order to achieve a more DRAMATIC effect you:
a) place each individually throughout the room
b) hang them on the wall allowing lots of space in between
c) group them together for more impact

2 Your den is already ECLECTIC, but you'd like it to be a touch more ROMANTIC. You...
a) add a few baskets of daisies
b) put a dimming mechanism on the lighting fixtures
c) place a hat on your bust of Beethoven

3 You have been elected to host a formal dinner in your otherwise NATURAL Setting. The CLASSIC finishing touch might be to replace the ceramic centerpiece with:
a) porcelain figurines
a) teakwood candlesticks
b) lucite fruit bowl

4 You walk into a country cottage parlor that boasts of a Sheraton side chair, a camelback sofa, upholstered in paisley, and an early 19th century French bookcase with verdigris finish. All that you would need to complete the desired "look" would be:
a) a weathervane
b) an abstract painting
c) English sporting prints

5 You'd like your bedroom to be ROMANTIC but have a little more DRAMATIC punch. You...
a) drape an embroidered shawl over your screen
b) you buy a black and white harlequin patterned bedspread
c) hang a birdcage from the ceiling

6 You're a NATURAL at heart, but you'd like your living area to be ECLECTIC in spirit. For your flooring you select:
a) a variety of oriental rugs
b) wall to wall carpeting
c) neutral hardwood

CROSSOVER DESIGN STYLES

DRAMATIC-NATURAL

CLASSIC-NATURAL

ROMANTIC-CLASSIC

ECLECTIC-ROMANTIC

COMMONLY ASKED QUESTIONS...
on Color, Style & Design

COLOR...

1) How do you decorate when you have more than one seasonal type (cool or warm person) living in the same home?

Color alliances exist within the four seasons and they are easy to see. There are four "compromise colors" that are correct for virtually everyone; a *soft white*...found in the summer palette, a *peachy-coral*...found in the spring palette, *aqua blue* found in summer's palette and *periwinkle blue* found in autumn's palette. All are foolproof and would be a good basis for family-room color schemes. You might ask yourself who spends the most time in a particular room and approach it that way. Or, what is the time of day when you are in that particular place. Try to get everyone living there involved and see if they can't go along with certain values of your favorite colors—the lightness or darkness—according to when you'll all be together or at least sharing that particular room. This is one way to get a seasonal compromise.

2) What about the impact of climate (such as sunlight) on color?

Sunlight can bleach out the intensity of any color. Certain colors such as strong pinks, yellows and greens prevail in the tropics, partly as a response to the bleaching of light. The light found in the desert also has somewhat the same effect. In northern climates where long winter days are bleak, bright colors—clear and vivid such as those found in winter's palette—are used to counteract the grimness. Regardless of where you live, you also need to take into consideration the position of your rooms: Do they face north or south? North light alters colors significantly, and a southern exposure warms and intensifies colors. These are major influences on the selection of the color you make for such large expanses as walls, window treatments and floorcoverings. When you are aware of the impact of your climate you will be forced to make the correct balance.

3) Do color preferences change during the course of a lifetime?

They may, but a switch doesn't mean you have to move out of your seasonal family. It is more likely that you will become interested in different tints or shades of what is already in your seasonal color palette. Because there are over 45 thousand colors already named and identified, it is doubtful that you will ever tire of your own Personal Palette. I also suggest that you paint an area of a wall that's out of general view and check it repeatedly for a few weeks. Check how your reactions change: 1) because you know it's there, and 2) because the variations of light in the room alter the way the room looks during the day. This is the safest way to try on a new color you are seriously considering using in large quantities.

STYLE...

4) How can I discover my own personal "look" from the four basic style types? (Classic, Dramatic, Romantic, Natural)

First, think about your likes and dislikes and make up a list. Now thumb through clothing catalogues and magazines noting the styles that say "you". Clip and keep a personal file of your favorite pictures. Take this file with you when you go shopping. Keep focused on your dominant basic look, even though you may choose to vary this look with one or more of the other three styles. That's just giving yourself that unique signature that's all your own.

5) What if I am really a 'Romantic' at heart but because of my professional work I must carry off a very 'Classic' style type?

Naturally you will have to abide by certain expected dress codes while working—'classic' usually being the most accepted. Consider a signature touch from your romantic preference in your selections: softer fabrics, lighter colors, a lace hanky or silk pocket square tucked into your blazer, a real flower boutonniere and so on. Naturally, on weekends and after work hours you can easily be your romantic self, varying your look for the occasion.

6) Do the four basic personal style types apply to everyone: men, women and children?

Absolutely! One of these four universal styles belongs to each of us. However, you must not forget to add your own unique signature along the way, depending upon your personal taste.

DESIGN...

7) *How would I integrate two design styles—for example: classic and dramatic?*

Assuming that your furniture is of a classic period style, it might be best to consider a change in the color scheme and fabric selection to make it more dramatic. Try brighter bolder colors and perhaps a geometric or large scale pattern for fabric-designated areas (sofas, chairs, tablecloths, stools, window treatments, walls, etc.). Refer to the dramatic sections of this book for further suggestions.

8) *My home is a hodge-podge of heirlooms and hand-me-downs that do not really fit the 'combination of design styles' known as 'Eclectic'. How can I establish this design favorite in my home, using what I already have?*

The true 'eclectic' is probably the most difficult look to achieve of the five basic and universal design groups. It requires practice, patience and understanding. Again, try thumbing through catalogues and magazines that feature your preferred decorating "look", as well as any of the items you already own in your home. Clip these and keep them in a file. Consider rearranging your possessions—one room at a time, trying the look for a few days or so. Ask a friend to help you. Consider hiring a design consultant to assist you in laying the groundwork by coming to your home for an hour of advice on what to do with your existing pieces. Try taking a home decorating class at your local adult education program.

9) *Should my preference in wardrobe style always be the same as my preference in decorating?*

Not necessarily. However, most of the time you will find that the two are mirror images—especially if you have a keen awareness of who you are and have come to develop your unique taste in the areas of style and design. For example, the person who feels most comfortable in classic clothing styles will undoubtedly select his/her furniture pieces and design style in the same classic vein, usually without even realizing the connection. Naturally, the person who understands *who they are* and *what they want* will make fewer mistakes, so the chances of everything being in harmony are that much greater for them.

SOURCE LISTING/CREDITS

ILLUSTRATIONS BY:
Anica Gibson-Style men/women, page 16
Joe Allen Hong-Flowers, pages 28,30,32,34,36
Dennis Redmond

INTERIOR RENDERINGS BY:
Anica Gibson, pages 48,66,72
David B. Redmond, pages 54,60
Special thanks to Chuck Winslow for his Eclectic Design, page 72

PHOTOGRAPHY BY:
Yvonne B. Lewis, pages 4,77

PICTURE CREDITS:
Cover-Montrachet and Solitaire Collections by Thomasville Furniture, T. Furniture,
Remembrance Collection by Waverly, Italianato & Pompadour by JP Stevens
Cool room-pg. 7; Prisms Sheet/Comforter by Andre Richard for Springmaid
Warm room-pg. 7; Iona Oak by Collier Campbell for JP Stevens
Traditional room pg.20, Petterson Associates Design Photography
Contemporary room pg. 20; Fascination Collection by Thomasville Furniture
Style Revell-ations-pg. 25, Beach House by Martex, Flowers; Petterson Associates Design
Photography, Painted Furniture-Woman's Day, Hachette Magazines, Inc.
Natural Profile, pg. 28, Back Country Collection by Waverly
Classic Profile, pg. 30, Petterson Associates Design Photography
Romantic Profile, pg.32, Wayside for Waverly Bed & Bath Collection
Dramatic Profile, pg. 34, Prestige Collection by Thomasville Furniture
Eclectic Profile pg. 36, Stone Creek Collection by Thomasville Furniture
Natural Bedroom, pg. 53, Country Inn-Shaker Plaid by JP Stevens
Natural Living Room pg. 53, Emporium-The Broadway, Northern California Stores
Classic Dining Room, pg. 59, Mahogany Collection, Thomasville Furniture
Classic Living Room, pg. 59, Emporium-The Broadway, Northern California Stores
Romantic Dining Room, pg. 65, Mary Rosie by Pat Farrel for Vintage Rose, Springmaid
Romantic Dining Room, pg. 65, American Oak Collection by Thomasville Furniture
Dramatic Bedroom, pg. 71, Ivy Lane Collection by Waverly
Dramatic Bedroom pg. 71, Petterson Associates Design Photography
Eclectic Living Room, pg. 77, Petterson Associates Design Photography
Eclectic Living Room, pg. 77, Yvonne B. Lewis Photography
Crossovers: Dramatic-Natural, pg. 82, Carousel Cellular-Night Mantle/Panorama, by
LouverDrape, a division of Home Fashions, Inc.
Classic-Natural, cover, pg. 82, Remembrance Collection, Waverly
Romantic-Classic, cover, pg. 83, Italianato & Pompadour by Louis Nichole for JP Stevens
Eclectic-Romantic, pg 83, Ivy Lane Collection by Waverly

FOR CONSUMER INFORMATION:

LouverDrape	1-800-421-6666
Martex Sheets	1-800-533-8229
Springmaid	1-800-537-0115
JP Stevens	1-800-533-8229
Thomasville	1-800-225-0265
Waverly	1-800-423-5881

FURNITURE STYLES

ADAM BROTHERS:
1760-1792
AMERICAN COLONIAL:
1620-1790
AMERICAN COUNTRY :
1960- present
AMERICAN FRONTIER:
1790-1890
ART DECO:
1908 - 1930
ART NOUVEAU:
1890 - 1905
ARTS & CRAFTS:
1900-1920
BAUHAUS:
1919-1925
BIEDERMEIER:
1815-1848
CHINESE:
1500-1800
CHIPPENDALE:
1740-1779
COLONIAL:
1700-1781
COMMONWEALTH:
1649-1660
DIRECTOIRE:
1795-1804
DUNCAN PHYFE:
1790-1830
DUTCH RENAISSANCE:
1500-1600
EARLY AMERICAN:
current
EASTLAKE:
1879-1895
EGYPTIAN:
4000-300 B.C.
ENGLISH REGENCY:
1793-1830

FEDERAL:
1795-1830
FRENCH COUNTRY:
13th century-present
FRENCH EMPIRE:
1804-1815
FRENCH PROVINCIAL:
1650-1900
FRENCH REGENCE:
1500-1600
FRENCH RENAISSANCE:
1453-1610
GEORGIAN:
1714-1795
GOTHIC:
1100-1500
GRAND RAPIDS:
1900-present
HEPPLEWHITE:
1770-1786
HIGH TECH:
1970's-present
HITCHCOCK STYLE:
1820-1850
INTERNATIONAL STYLE:
1950's
ITALIAN PROVINCIAL:
1700-1850
ITALIAN RENAISSANCE:
1400-1600
JACOBEAN:
1603-1649
LATE COLONIAL:
1700-1790
LOUIS XIII:
1610-1643
LOUIS XIV:
1643-1715
LOUIS XV:
1723-1774
LOUIS XVI:
1774-1793

MEDITERRANEAN:
16th century-present
MEMPHIS:
1981-present
MISSION:
1895-1910
MODERN:
1925-present
MODERN METAL:
current
ORIENTAL:
modern-current
PENNSYLVANIA DUTCH:
1680-1850
QUEEN ANNE:
1702-1715
RANCH STYLE:
1950's-present
SCANDINAVIAN:
1930's-present

SHAKER:
1776-1850
SHERATON:
1780-1806
SOUTHWEST:
1970's-present
SPANISH RENAISSANCE:
1500-1700
TUDOR-ELIZABETHAN:
1509-1603
URBAN PRIMITIVE:
current
UTILITY:
1939-1947
VICTORIAN:
1830-1890
WILLIAM AND MARY:
1689-1702

COLOR GLOSSARY

PRIMARY COLORS: Red, Yellow and Blue
SECONDARY COLORS: Orange, Green and Violet
TERTIARY COLORS: A mixture containing equal parts of a primary color and its neighboring color
HUE: A pure, bright color as seen in the primary and secondary colors
VALUE: The lightness or darkness of a color determined by tinting (adding white) or shading (adding black)
INTENSITY: The strength or vividness of a hue; the brightness or dullness of a color
TINT: White added to the color, thereby making it appear light or paler
SHADE: Black added to the color, thereby making it appear darker or muted
COOL COLOR: A touch of blue (or green or violet) added to a color
WARM COLOR: A touch of yellow (or red or orange) added to a color
TONE: Adding both black and white to the color, thereby lessening its intensity or "toning" it down
COMPLEMENTARY COLORS: A relationship and combination that is created with two colors that are found directly across from one another in the color spectrum—e.g. red and green, blue and orange, yellow and violet

DISCOVER YOUR PERSONAL STYLE

To receive your FREE Style Analysis with the purchase of your Personal Style Kit, complete the easy questions below.

YOUR PERSONAL STYLE ANALYSIS QUESTIONNAIRE

Please read every question carefully and check the answer that best describes you. Since this is a very personalized analysis, it's important that you answer **all** questions.

In order to answer all questions accurately, you'll need these items:

- A full length mirror
- Pencil and paper
- Hair pulled back away from face
- If possible, a friend or family member to help you (it's often difficult to be objective about oneself)

If you have 1 or 2 color photos of yourself in natural daylight (i.e. Polaroid), include them with your completed questionnaire. All photos will be returned to you promptly with your style anlaysis.

---

1. **My Personal Style type (as learned in Chapter 1) is:**
   A ☐ CLASSIC (also known as: Elegant, Traditional, Tailored, Conservative, Sophisticated, Formal)
   B ☐ DRAMATIC (also known as: Glamorous, Exotic, Creative, Theatrical, Artistic, Sexy)
   C ☐ NATURAL (also known as: Casual, Sporty, Informal, Country, Outdoorsy, Basic)
   D ☐ ROMANTIC (also known as: (Feminine, Ingenue, Soft, Victorian, Delicate, Poetic)

2. **The selection that best describes my personality is:**
   A ☐ Soft, charming and supportive
   B ☐ Free-spirited, energetic, friendly
   C ☐ Understated, practical, poised
   D ☐ Independent, stimulating, flamboyant

3. **The woman whose personal style I most admire is:**
   A ☐ Cher
   B ☐ Goldie Hawn
   C ☐ Jackie (Kennedy) Onassis
   D ☐ Jane Seymour

4. **The selection that best describes my clothing preference is:**
   A ☐ Comfortable/loose
   B ☐ Tailored/fitted
   C ☐ Architectural/contrasted
   D ☐ Detailed/frilly

5. **The selection that best describes my preference in line design is:**
   A ☐ Sharp/angular
   B ☐ Swirled/curled
   C ☐ Solid/straight
   D ☐ Waved/watered

6. **The selection that best describes my fabric preference is:**
   A ☐ Soft, drapey, flowing
   B ☐ Easy-care, natural
   C ☐ Shiny, ornate, unusual
   D ☐ Woven, smooth, matte-finish

7. **My lifework (as discussed in chapter 2) is:**
   A ☐ Student
   B ☐ Working Single
   C ☐ Homemaker/Single
   D ☐ Working mother
   E ☐ Work in office
   F ☐ Work at home
   G ☐ Work as a volunteer
   H ☐ Other _____

8. **My age group is:**
   A ☐ Under 25   D ☐ 46-55
   B ☐ 25-35   E ☐ 56 and over
   C ☐ 36-45

9. **Other than for work, I dress up for special occasions each week approximately:**
   A ☐ once a week   D ☐ four-five times
   B ☐ twice weekly   E ☐ five or more times
   C ☐ three times weekly F ☐ None or seldom

If you wish to retain this page, please send a photocopy of same.

10. My body type (as learned in Chapter 3) is best described as:
   A ☐ Hourglass
   B ☐ Triangle
   C ☐ Inverted Triangle
   D ☐ Rectangle

11. My face shape (as learned in Chapter 4) is best described as:
   A ☐ Round
   B ☐ Square
   C ☐ Triangular
   D ☐ Inverted Triangle
   E ☐ Rectangle
   F ☐ Oval

12. The selection that best describes my favorite colors is:
   A ☐ Pastels and tints
   B ☐ Neutrals and muted
   C ☐ Subdued and earthy
   D ☐ Bold and contrasting

13. My Seasonal Color type (as learned in Chapter 5) is:
   A ☐ Spring (warm colors)
   B ☐ Summer (cool colors)
   C ☐ Autumn (warm colors)
   D ☐ Winter (cool colors)
   E ☐ Unknown

14. The selection that best describes my makeup preference is:
   A ☐ Vivid
   B ☐ Polished
   C ☐ Delicate
   D ☐ Minimal

15. The selection that best describes my hairstyle preference is:
   A ☐ Carefree or straight
   B ☐ Timeless and neat
   C ☐ Soft curls or feathered
   D ☐ Geometric or striking

16. The selection that best describes my fragrance preference is:
   A ☐ Floral
   B ☐ Woodsy
   C ☐ Oriental
   D ☐ Spicy

17. Additional comments on my characteristics

   _____
   _____
   _____
   _____
   _____

FREE STYLE ANALYSIS
with your purchase of a Revelli Personal Style Kit

WARDROBE PLAN

SKIRTS JACKETS DRESSES

REVELLI

Classic PERSONAL STYLE KIT

Revelli Style Kit includes:
- An individual wardrobe plan with illustrations in your best styles
- Tips on which clothes, accessories, makeup and hairstyles to wear for your personal style type.
- A list of your best styles by designer label.
- Body and face shape guidelines for your specific type.

GUIDELINES FOR FACE/BODY SHAPE

CLASSIC

TYPE DESIGNERS LABEL GUIDE

MAKEUP HAIR ACCESSORY

TIPS

See order form on page 94 for cost (C & D)

DISCOVER YOUR BEST COLORS

To receive your FREE Color Analysis with the purchase of your seasonal color kit, complete the easy questions below.

YOUR PERSONAL COLOR ANALYSIS QUESTIONNAIRE

Please read every question carefully and check the answer that best describes you. Since this is a very personalized analysis, it's important that you answer all questions. Take special care when answering questions about skin tone since your season is based primarily on your skin tone.

In order to answer the questions accurately, you'll need these items:
- natural daylight (not fluorescent light)
- a sheet of 8½ × 11" white paper
- a mirror large enough to reflect your face and hair
- a family member or friend to help you (it's often difficult to be objective about oneself)

If you have 1 or 2 color photos (i.e. Polaroid), of yourself in natural daylight include them with your completed questionnaire. All photos will be returned to you promptly with your color anlaysis.

SKIN COLOR

Your skin will fall into one of the following categories: very fair, light, medium or dark. It may also have a specific tint such as pink, peach or yellow. In each of the questions below check the answers that describes your skin as closely as possible.

For question 1, hold your forearm over the white paper with the inner side of your wrist facing up. This is the best area for determining your natural skin tone.

1. **How would you best describe your skin tone?**
   A ☐ Olive (light, medium, dark), black
   B ☐ Light beige with a pink tinge
   C ☐ Rosy pink, deep pink
   D ☐ Red rose-beige, gray beige
   E ☐ Ivory
   F ☐ Peach, peach-beige, peach-pink
   G ☐ Golden beige, coppery beige, golden black, tawny

2. **What is your basic skin color?**
   A ☐ Very fair
   B ☐ Light
   C ☐ Medium
   D ☐ Dark

3. **Do you have a sallow (yellowish) cast to your skin?**
   A ☐ Yes   B ☐ No

4. **When I tan my skin turns:**
   A ☐ Golden brown
   B ☐ Red
   C ☐ Bronze or copper brown
   D ☐ Berry brown (dark brown)

HAIR COLOR

5. **What color was your hair when you were 9 or 10 years old?**
   A ☐ White blond (towhead)
   B ☐ Ash blond
   C ☐ Yellow or golden blond
   C ☐ Light brown
   E ☐ Medium brown
   F ☐ Dark brown
   G ☐ Red or auburn
   H ☐ Black

6. **How would you best describe your natural hair color today?**
   A ☐ Blue-black or brown (med. to dark)
   B ☐ Ash or smoky blond
   C ☐ Smoky brown
   D ☐ Platinum (no golden highlights)
   E ☐ Blue-gray
   F ☐ Red, chestnut, auburn, golden honey-blond, golden honey-brown, copper brown
   G ☐ Yellow-blond, strawberry-blond, golden brown, blond-red, golden gray
   H ☐ Salt and pepper, silver-gray, white (snow)

7. **The color of my hair when I look in the mirror today is:**
   A ☐ Light   B ☐ Medium   C ☐ Dark

8. **What color are the natural highlights (sheen) in your hair today?**
   A ☐ Ash blond   D ☐ Golden yellow
   B ☐ Red   E ☐ Gray
   C ☐ Blue-black   F ☐ None

9. **Do you color your hair?**
   A ☐ Yes   B ☐ No

If you wish to retain these questionnaire pages, please send a photocopy of same.

92

EYE COLOR

10. My eye color is: A ☐ Light   B ☐ Medium   C ☐ Dark

11. Which color best describes your eyes?
    A ☐ Blue   B ☐ Green   C ☐ Aqua   D ☐ Gray-blue   E ☐ Hazel   F ☐ Gray
    G ☐ Brown   H ☐ Black

12. Do your eyes change color depending on what you're wearing?   A ☐ Yes   B ☐ No

13. Which group of colors do you like the best?
    (Make your selection based on the group of colors, not on an individual color.)
    A ☐ Pure white, pure black, charcoal gray, true red, royal blue; burgundy, dark navy
    B ☐ Soft white, rose brown, pearl gray, mauve, pastel blue, soft lavender
    C ☐ Oyster white, dark brown, rust, olive green, teal blue, gold, camel
    D ☐ Peach, ivory, turquoise, apricot, golden brown, bright clear yellow, medium blue,
       clear yellow green

14. What intensity of colors do you prefer?
    A ☐ Soft pastels or tints   B ☐ Bold, strong and primary   C ☐ Clear, vivid and warm
    D ☐ Muted, earthy, naturals

15. My family heritage is: A ☐ _____
                              B ☐ I am unsure of my family origins

16. I have been color analyzed and my season is: _____

17. Additional comments on my characteristics: _____
    _____

FREE COLOR ANALYSIS
with your purchase of a REVELLI SEASONAL COLOR KIT

Revelli Color Kit includes:
- Wallet size Personal Palette with fabric swatches in your best colors.
- How to use your best colors for wardrobe, accessories and cosmetics.
- For women, a list of your best colors from national brand cosmetics: foundation, blusher, eye shadow and lipstick.

See order form on page 94 for cost (A & B)

REVELLI ORDER FORM

My Seasonal Color group is: (Please circle one)
SPRING   SUMMER   AUTUMN   WINTER   UNKNOWN

MY Personal Style type is:
CLASSIC   DRAMATIC   NATURAL   ROMANTIC   UNKNOWN

☐ I am enclosing the Style ☐ Color ☐ questionnaire(s) on pgs. 90-93
☐ Please send me the items checked on the Revelli order form below:

1 ☐ COLOR ANALYSIS QUESTIONNAIRE—**FREE** (with the purchase of a Revelli Color Kit) for anyone unsure of their seasonal color type. See COLOR KIT #2 below.

2 ☐ COLOR KIT—Wallet size Revelli Personal Palette with fabric swatches in your best colors, tips on how to wear your colors in wardrobe, accessories, make-up and a national brands haircolor shades and cosmetics list in your best colors (circle season above or refer to #1)...$21.00

3 ☐ ALL FOUR SEASONAL COLOR KITS (Save $25!)....................$59.00

4 ☐ STYLE ANALYSIS QUESTIONNAIRE—**FREE** (with the purchase of a Revelli Style Kit) for anyone unsure of their personal style type. See STYLE KIT #5 below.

5 ☐ STYLE KIT—Your individual wardrobe plan featuring clothing illustrations designed for your personality, lifestyle and body type. Includes tips on what clothes and accessories suit your personal style type plus additional tips on how to create your own individual statement (circle style type above or refer to #4)................$21.00

6 ☐ ALL FOUR PERSONAL STYLE KITS (Save $25!)....................$59.00

7 ☐ BOOK— Clare Revelli's best-selling DESIGN & YOU, *Your Guide To Decorating With Style*..$9.50

8 ☐ BOOK— Clare Revelli's best-selling COLOR & YOU, *A Guide To Discovering Your Best Colors*—for men and women $7.50

9 ☐ BOOK— Clare Revelli's best-selling STYLE & YOU, *Every Woman's Guide to Total Style*...$7.50

10 ☐ BOOK—THE COLORS OF YOUR LIFE by Clare Revelli for Clairol The definitive full-color seasonal haircolor book includes a complimentary skintone analyzer, make-up lists, national brand haircolor shades by season, color palettes and more ! $12.00

11 ☐ PALETTE CARDS—A seasonal color card for each of the four seasons, 20 colors per card plus make-up suggestions. Set of four.......................$5.00

12 ☐ SKIN TONE ANALYZER—Precision skin tone analysis tool.......$4.00

Sub-total _____

CA residents add sales tax _____

Total amount enclosed _____

All prices include postage and handling. Discounts available for quantity orders.
(For more information,write or call Revelli : 415-673-6313)
If you wish to retain this page, please send a photocopy of same.

Please print clearly:

My season is _____ My style is _____

NAME _____

ADDRESS _____

CITY _____ STATE _____ ZIP_____

Enclosed is a check money order (*payable to REVELLI*)
Charge to my MASTERCARD/VISA (minimum charge $10.00)

Card #: _____

Phone (*required for all charge orders*) : _____

Signature: _____ exp. date: _____

I am a(n): ☐ image/color consultant ☐ salon ☐ educator

Send to: **REVELLI** • 1850 UNION STREET
               SAN FRANCISCO, CA 94123 • 415-673-6313
               If you wish to retain this page, please send a photocopy of same.

95

DECORATE LIKE A PRO!

Design Your Home In Your Own Personal Style

The Revelli HOME DECORATING KIT offers a design style for everyone – featuring the five basic types discussed in the DESIGN & YOU book.

Choose from NATURAL, CLASSIC, DRAMATIC, ROMANTIC, or ECLECTIC ... only $29.95 each. Select three or more kits at $19.95 each or the complete set of all five kits for $89.95.

Each REVELLI HOME DECORATING KIT includes:

■ DESIGN & YOU book ... Your Guide To Decorating With Style by Clare Revelli.

■ REVELLI ROOM DESIGN PLANNER . . . an easy step-by-step guide to designing and redecorating your home. Includes vinyl layout grid, scale ruler, reusable peel/stick furniture and accessory symbols.

■ BEAUTIFUL BOTANICAL FLORAL PRINT ... in full color, suitable for framing, 8" x 10" size.

■ PERSONAL PALETTE COLOR CARDS ... great guidelines for wardrobe and home decorating decisions. Each kit includes the complete set of four color cards featuring 80 colors.

■ DESIGN STYLE LETTER . . . a three-page personalized letter from Clare Revelli. Packed with terrific tips on your colors, style and design tastes to help you begin your decorating scheme.

Please send me the following REVELLI HOME DECORATING KITS(S).

☐ NATURAL   ☐ CLASSIC   ☐ ROMANTIC   ☐ DRAMATIC   ☐ ECLECTIC

at a cost of $29.95 each (+ $4 for s/h), or 3 or more kits at $19.95 each (+$7 s/h). Order all five kits for $89.95 (+$8 s/h).

Please complete the order form on page 95 (see reverse) and return to REVELLI

If you wish to retain this page, please send a photocopy of same.